I0470931

Farming with Family Ain't Always Easy.

CHANGING HOW YOUR FAMILY BUSINESS DEALS WITH CHANGE

Mark Andrew Junkin

Dedication

This book is dedicated to keeping your family's name on your farm's mailbox for another 100 years.

Mark Andrew Junkin
www.farmsuccession.com

"Farming With Family Ain't Always Easy!"

To buy books in quantity for corporate use or incentives call
800-474-2057 or chairman@farmsuccession.com

Download Kindle book at amazon.com
Listen to audio book version on iTunes

Third Edition - Copyright © 2017 by Mark Andrew Junkin

ALL RIGHTS RESERVED. No part of this book may be reproduced
or transmitted in any form by any means, electronic or
mechanical, including photocopying and recording, or by an
information storage and retrieval system, except as may be
expressly permitted in writing from the publisher. Requests for
permission should be addressed to Agriculture Strategy, P.O. Box
312 Solon, IA 52333.

"Farming With Family Ain't Always Easy!"

Table of Contents

Introduction: The Science of Farm Decision Making

When I was in Agriculture College, I dated a sweet girl who was majoring in sport psychology. I had never heard of this academic field, so I asked her what it was.

She said that sport psychology teaches you how to get into an athlete's head in order to get the most out of him, and to optimize his interactions with his teammates. Years ago, before coaches started using sports psychology, professional basketball players used to get into bench-clearing brawls on the court and fights in the locker room because these world-class athletes had larger-than-life egos. They had the talent, but they didn't know how to work together to win. In the 1960s, second-class franchises with third-class athletes started winning championships because their coaches started to using sport psychology. What they may have lacked in skill, they made up for in teamwork. My girlfriend at the time went on to explain that business was starting to use the principles of sport psychology to get the most from their management teams—and that was exactly what she was going to do.

I looked at her and said, "But what does psychology have to do with growing corn?" I looked at her psychology degree as being absolutely useless.

It wasn't until I went home to my father's farm that it hit me: you can be the smartest farmer in the world, but if you can't get everyone pulling in the same direction, agricultural knowledge and skills go to waste. I suddenly realized that her degree psychology was more useful for farming than my own agriculture degree.

"Farming With Family Ain't Always Easy!"

How often do you see two brothers split up an operation because they can't get along? Then how often do they both struggle because they lose their economies of scale and take on ridiculous debt loads?

The key to long-term success is to have everyone use the same internal compass driving them toward shared goals. When families have different destinations in mind and different ideas of how to get there, tempers flare, feelings get hurt, and the business suffers. Soft issues become hard problems. Sadly, most farmers don't realize there is a problem until it's too late.

My name is Mark Andrew Junkin (Andy). I am a seventh-generation farmer, a professional mediator, and an executive coach from Bobcaygeon, Ontario, Canada. My own family had serious problems with farm management and succession, which led my parents to divorce. Since then, I have dedicated myself to changing how succession planning is done. I run a niche agricultural consulting practice where I work face-to-face with farmers throughout the world either in person or via Skype. As a professional mediator, I help farm families prevent and solve farm succession crises.

In addition to my mediation work, I am the author of a syndicated monthly column for a growing number of farm papers across North America and Australia, and I also speak at conferences and other events. In my work, I've come across families in desperate need of help. My track record for teaching people how to turn their family and their business around speaks for itself. Although I get called in during a crisis, my life's purpose is to prevent disasters before they happen. This book outlines my unique approach to helping farm families make decisions together.

I want to help you think about how your family makes decisions and attempt to inspire you to take some simple steps to improve how your family works together.

"Farming With Family Ain't Always Easy!"

This book is written by a farmer for farmers and will use specific farming examples, but the tools and techniques in it can apply to any family business. All the stories I tell in this book are true, however, the names of people and identifying features have been changed to protect their privacy.

Speaking of stories, although many of the ones in this book feature men, it's very important to understand that they could easily feature women. On some farms, matriarchs call all the shots and daughters are first in line to take over.

This book isn't just about farm succession; it's also about dealing with change. There are three central topics:

Motivation: What drives us to get out of bed on a daily basis?

Fears: What behaviors cause families to "go off track?"

Processes: What things can you do to stay on track?

In the final section of this book, I will introduce a simple management concept called "Rock, Paper, Scissors."

Rock: What are the stones you can take out of your family business' shoes?

Paper: How do you build a roadmap for success that everyone can use?

Scissors: How can you continually cut the fat from your operation?

These concepts can turn around the most complex family business situation and get everyone pulling in the same direction.

"Farming With Family Ain't Always Easy!"

Chapter 1: Gaining the Competitive Edge

Edward Deming was a statistician, a professor, and an all-around brilliant guy. You've probably never heard of him, but he transformed the manufacturing business model in Japan and nearly brought down the American automobile industry.

Deming believed that a good business strategy wasn't enough to make a business profitable. What put one business ahead of the rest was management's ability to convert that strategy into action. In other words, Deming studied change. He was the only one who combined strategic planning, management systems, problem solving, and psychology into a unique bundle of ideas. Until Deming, wishy-washy things like psychology really had nothing to do with "real man" activities, like building cars.

Deming went to General Motors (GM) in the 1950s and said that he wanted to improve the efficiency of every worker—from the boardroom to the shop floor—by teaching him better problem solving techniques. The executives at GM thought it was hilarious that a nerdy guy with a bowtie wanted to go into the factory and tell the boys how to build cars. Deming was asked to leave.

GM and Deming seemed to be speaking different languages. So Deming went to Japan where they really spoke different languages. The difference was the Japanese listened to him and got it. In the end, Deming helped transform a little company called Toyota into a world automobile giant.

Deming helped Toyota excel at setting goals, working together to achieve them, and developing problem-solving techniques when things went wrong. In other words, he evolved their ability to proactively change. Thanks to Deming's ideas, Toyota was able to build higher quality cars faster and cheaper than anyone else in the business.

"Farming With Family Ain't Always Easy!"

GM may have mocked his approach, but Deming almost put the American automobile industry under by improving the way Toyota managed change. Deming's principles have never yet been applied to farming, or to most family business sectors, but they are just as relevant today as they were 60 years ago.

When we think of the family farm, we think of the romantic image of a farmer and his pre-teenage children. We think of 4-H calves, families baling hay and big thanksgiving dinners.

However, the family farm is really a business run by multiple persons with different perspectives and philosophies. There comes a time in every farm's history when the family farm actually becomes a real business. The kids are no longer just teenagers who gleefully do what Dad says; they are adults with their own needs, ideas, and visions. The farm evolves from a one-man show to a family operation with multiple partners.

Although we try to be neighborly, farming is really a competition for land. Every farmer can access the same inputs, advice, and machinery. The true difference between two farms is the quality of the decisions each family makes and how well farmers implement good ideas.

Farmers haven't really thought about the science of farm decision-making and its impact on the farm's bottom line and long-term strategic success. It's time to think about how change impacts the viability of a farm business. Improving the quality of decision-making directly increases profitability, reduces risks, and drastically improves family business relations. It significantly reduces stress and yields higher rates of sustainable strategic growth.

You can be the smartest farmer in the world, but it matters very little if you can't get your family to agree to your concepts, and make those ideas a reality. Money will slip through the cracks if

"Farming With Family Ain't Always Easy!"

you have a dysfunctional business culture and can't execute good decisions.

Will you give your own farm the competitive edge, or wait for your neighbors to do it first? Will your neighbor own your land in 20 years, or will your sons and daughters?

Toyota almost put GM into bankruptcy because Toyota's management system had a real competitive edge. This wasn't due to their economies of scale or other factors. It was due to the superiority of their business culture that is something we've never discussed before in Farming.

The real question is what neighbor is going to adapt these management advantages and have a more efficient farm? Will your family own your farm or will your neighbors? It all depends on your actions today.

Evolving how you function as an organization not only improves profitability but also makes farming with family fun again.

"Farming With Family Ain't Always Easy!"

Chapter 2: The Decade of Dysfunction

We all know that farm succession planning usually happens in an accountant's office. The trouble is, accountants tend to focus on avoiding taxes and pay only lip service to the transition of management. Signing paperwork at the accountant's office represents only 10 minutes of the farm's history when in reality, the father and son could have been working as partners for over a decade. For a lot of families, these years aren't rosy, and for many it's downright dysfunctional. That's why I call the decade when the parents and children are co-managing a family business "the decade of dysfunction."

The root of farm succession problems isn't limited to the transfer of assets. It's the emotional issues created by a decade of a frustrated family trying to work together. The father is probably used to running the farm autocratically. As younger family members join the family business, the style of management should gradually adjust so that all the partners are included in the decision-making process.

Many families have problems with this transition. Parents need to learn that how they interacted with their kids when they were teenagers should be different from how they interact with them as adults and business partners. Without this transition, tensions and resentments will build within both generations.

The transition from a sole proprietor (do-what-Dad-says) mentality to a multiple-partner, multiple-generation, and often multiple-sibling business relationship is tough. The challenge isn't how to divide the assets on paper, but how to manage the business together and gradually transfer management control from one generation to the next.

For most farm families, the impacts of miscommunication and stubborn egos during the "dysfunctional decade" affect the

"Farming With Family Ain't Always Easy!"

farm's bottom line more than the impacts of the markets and weather combined.

For many farmers and small business owners, Dad is the boss. He is a sole proprietor and the farm is his kingdom where everyone does what he or she is told. It's as if Dad is a downhill skier. It's just him and the hill. He decides how and when to move his body, when to turn left or right, when to slow down and when to tuck to get down the hill the fastest.

For Dad, farming with his family is like changing sports. It's like going from downhill skiing to playing basketball. Different game, different rules. Most patriarchs don't understand the rules of the new game and often haven't even realized that they have changed sports.

When I first played "Aussie Rules" football, I didn't get the concept of the sport and my first game was brutal. I was often offside and got hit unexpectedly several times. As a mediator, I see a lot of farm patriarchs with kids in their 20s who feel emotionally bruised like I physically was. Dads simply need someone to teach them the rules of the game and then coach them into being good team players.

Once they realize that the game has changed, some parents may still try to be the player, coach, referee, and team captain all at the same time. They think they know the rules to the game, but really they still have a lot to learn.

For Moms and Dads who have created empires, one of the toughest challenges of their lifetime is letting go of control and teaching management to the next generation.

I often say that any fool can teach his son how to drive a tractor straight and leave it to him bought and paid for. Few can teach their kids management skills so that the next time those kids need

"Farming With Family Ain't Always Easy!"

to buy a tractor, they are in such a good strategic position that they can afford to buy two.

What is the sense in a man working his entire life to build a family empire if it crumbles shortly after his funeral? Change is tough, but it's necessary if your family business is going to survive for 50 years.

Most fathers will insist that their farm is the family's farm, but their "my way or the highway" mentality suggests it's not a family farm at all—it's a one-man empire.

Every patriarch needs to ask himself: Is this a family farm or is it a one-man empire? The answer can mark a major milestone in the farm's history and determine its future. Any man can die and leave his farm to his kids in his will. Few men successfully pass on their business acumen. That's why it's rare to see farming empires that are still commercially viable after 30 years.

If Dad is truly intent on building a family farm, he has to realize that he must put his ego aside and put his family's needs first. It's tough to let go of the decision- making and deal with the fear of being sidelined.

For example, many family patriarchs enjoy controlling the company checkbook and tend to keep the farm's financial affairs a secret. As they get older, even as they pass over the daily responsibilities (the brawn) of the farm to their sons or daughters, they hold onto control of the money (the brains) to their grave. When the father dies, the children are left wondering how money was made and spent. They may have seen their father purchase equipment in the past, but they lack the depth of knowledge about how to make that equipment return the investment. Most successful farmers are "doers," not "teachers." Unfortunately business sense can't be learned by osmosis. It's something a father has to teach.

"Farming With Family Ain't Always Easy!"

Ironically, farm kids have the common sense not to fight for the wheel of a truck as it's going down the dirt concession at 80 miles per hour, but most of them struggle for control of the business. Quite often their ignorance sends the business fishtailing, and too often, it sends it into the ditch.

"I don't know what is going on in Dad's head." A 33-year-old dairy farmer was struggling to take over the operation after his dad had been diagnosed with cancer. The older the father got, the more secretive he became about the farm's financials. He wanted to keep his role on the farm and his status in the family. The father had a "go, go, go" personality and had little patience for teaching his son what he thought his son should have known by now. But the son was going to have a stroke, if his father didn't start teaching him what he knew.

Whether your family is "stuck in a ditch" or you are "sailing down the road," every family can benefit from improving the quality of joint decision-making. By improving how decisions are made, farming remains a rational instead of emotional business that is focused on profit and long-term success, not a battle of egos.

Speaking of egos, in families with multiple siblings, who becomes the next chief executive officer (CEO) of the farm is too often based on gender rather than merit. Although many farms are splitting equity equally amongst siblings, rarely does a farm corporation have a daughter as CEO unless there aren't any male heirs. The daughter is often excluded from strategic conversations. She may work 60 hours a week on the farm, but her father never really treats her as a full partner. She will have an even steeper learning curve if she is left to run the farm after Dad dies. Leaving a farm to a male heir was the cultural norm for generations. It's going to take generations to change that mindset, but change it must. You can start doing it on your farm today by changing the way you and your family make decisions together.

"Farming With Family Ain't Always Easy!"

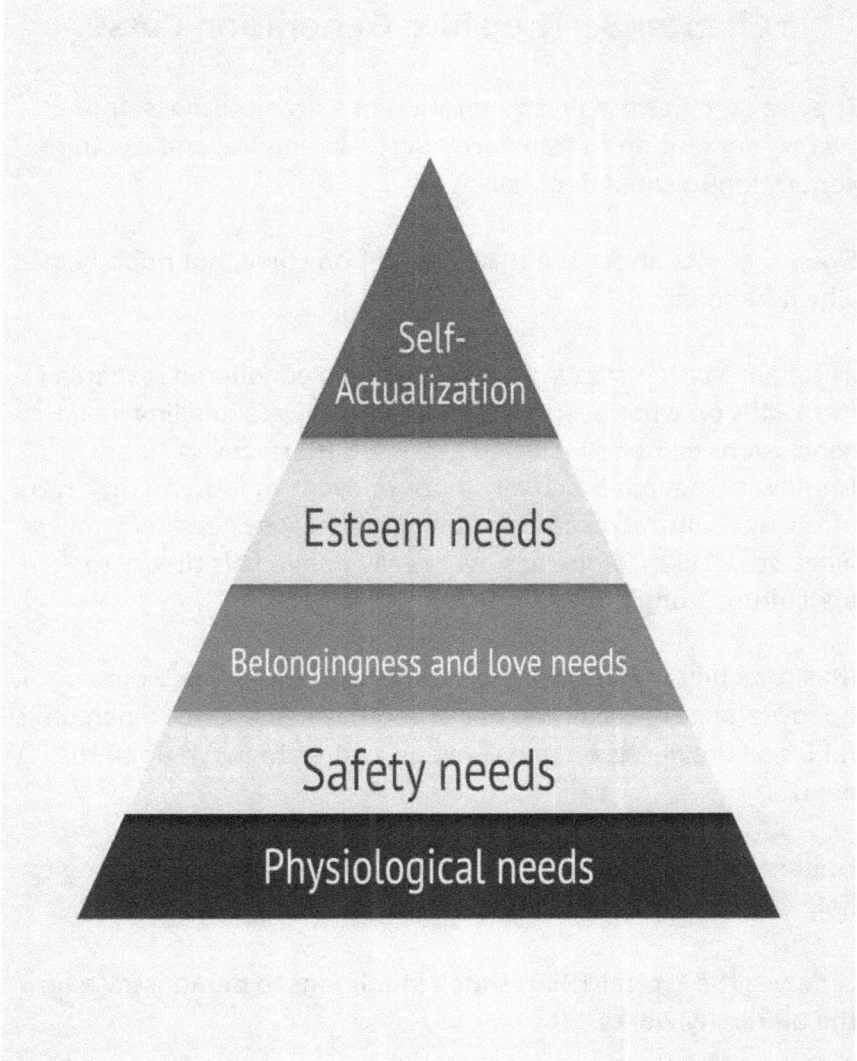

IMAGE 1: MASLOW'S HIERARCHY OF NEEDS

Chapter 3: The Third Generation Curse

They say it takes the first generation to start a business, the second generation to transform it into an empire, and the third generation to squander it all away.

Everyone talks about the third generation curse, but nobody asks why it happens.

Abraham Maslow was a psychologist who conducted research in the 1940s on what every person needs to live a fulfilling life. His conclusions came to be called Maslow's Hierarchy of Needs. Maslow's research is actually more relevant to farming than most of the agricultural research of the time because Maslow studied what drives us. No one has ever really applied his theory to agriculture—until now.

Maslow's hierarchy consists of five levels (see Image 1 on opposite page). Each level has different needs. Once a person fulfills all the needs on one level, he aspires to move up to the next.

Understanding Maslow's Hierarchy and applying it to farming can help you motivate people and make your farm a success.

Let's use the typical 1950s Dutch immigrant to demonstrate how the hierarchy works.

We'll begin with the first generation immigrant. Much of Holland starved during World War II, and a lot of kids ate tulip bulbs in order to survive. "Never again will we starve," one Dutchman said to me—and he meant it.

After WWII, many Dutch came to Canada with nothing but a few dollars in their shoes. They worked as laborers on their sponsor's farms, where many were treated inhumanely. They were

"Farming With Family Ain't Always Easy!"

motivated to work their tails off just to put roofs over their heads and meals on their tables.

These immigrants were at Level 1 of Maslow's Hierarchy, physiological needs. The goals of those on Level 1 are similar to the goals of someone who has been dropped off in the woods. He has to use his survival skills to build a shelter, clothe himself and scrounge for his next meal.

Once the Level 1 needs were met, the Dutch immigrants refocused all their efforts to making sure they never starved again. In other words, they moved on to Level 2, safety needs.

In our example, safety meant stashing away and investing as much cash as they could so that they would feel safe in the future and never had to "just survive" again.

To a European in the 1950s, safety meant owning a 100-acre farm. The war made once-reliable government bonds worthless overnight. A man who owned land could grow food for his family and sell some farm produce, so investing in farmland was the safest thing he could do.

Once he met his need for safety, the first generation Dutch Canadian focused on building a family and a community. This marked a shift up to Level 3, belongingness and love needs also known as social needs.

Many Dutch came to Canada as bachelors and they were lonely. They lived in shacks as laborers on farms and all they did was work. In order to meet their social needs, many returned briefly to Holland, brought back a wife to Canada, and then focused on building a family.

The other way they fulfilled their social needs was through the church. Since many didn't speak English well and had few friends, Sundays at church became the centre of their social life.

"Farming With Family Ain't Always Easy!"

Once they built a community for themselves, many first-generation immigrant farmers were content to live the rest of their lives at Level 3. Family was their top priority, closely followed by the church.

Now let's look at their children, the second generation Dutch Canadian. Since their fathers had taken care of Level 1 (physiological) and Level 2 (safety) for them, second generation farmers started out at Maslow's Level 3, social needs. Like their fathers, family was their priority, and many men fathered six or more children. This generation, too, wanted to grow a family nucleus in their new country and to make their church the center of their social world.

Once they had finished building their families and their communities, these second-generation farmers set their sights on Level 4, esteem needs. At this point, everything they did was to gain the respect and admiration of their friends and neighbors.

High-end vehicles fill the parking lots of Catholic or Christian Reform Churches these days—the churches of choice for many Dutch Canadians. It's common for the men inside to say that they're plowing down the original farmhouses and building new $500,000 homes. Fifty years ago, anyone who bought a luxury car instead of paying off the farm mortgage would have been called a fool. That is because back in the 1960s, the Dutch Canadians were focused on safety, not how successful they appeared to be.

So why did the second-generation take risks to grow and expand? It wasn't because of a change in religious doctrine, but because their needs had evolved. Second-generation farmers, unlike their fathers, moved up the hierarchy to Level 4, esteem. And believe it or not, many of these men can attribute their success to coffee after church on Sundays.

After church these guys talked with one another about business. What started as a friendly chat became a competition to see who

"Farming With Family Ain't Always Easy!"

could grow faster. In other words, their egos drove the farm's growth.

Some families that started with $400 in the 1950s are worth over $15,000,000 today. They could have quit growing years ago, but the drive for esteem motivated them to expand so that they could brag about their success during coffee at church. Esteem is an incredibly powerful force.

Esteem is a double-edged sword. It can be a really good motivator, as it was for many second-generation farmers, but it can also kill motivation all together.

When a third generation child grows up with survival, security, and social needs already met, all that's left to focus on is Level 4, esteem. The problem with being driven only by a need for esteem is that sometimes it tempts people to live beyond their business and personal means. The fierce competition to outdo neighbors can override rational thought. Farmers who focus on impressing other people stop making strategic decisions based on return-on-investment and start growing the farm at any cost. Being esteem-hungry creates stupid farmers.

John: The Man who thought he was King

Tim was a second-generation Dutch Canadian, and one of the most successful hog farmers in Ontario. Tim's Dad Matthias had gotten his start as a tobacco farmer and Tim had invested the farm's government buyout in the hog industry. Tim worked hard all his life and eventually built an empire.

Tim's son John, on the other hand, grew up having everything handed to him on a silver platter. He lived in an enormous house, wore name brand clothing and never did without.

John was 23 when he told me that he owned and ran a thousand head farrow-to-finish barn. When John went to set up his

"Farming With Family Ain't Always Easy!"

corporation and build his barn, the banks begged for his business. The vice-president of a major bank even came to see him. John thought the VP was coming because he was such a fantastic manager, but it was really because of his dad's wealth and reputation.

John's ego gave him a false and dangerous sense of Entitlement. He believed that the bank had just loaned him the money to build such a big barn because he was such a good guy. He felt like he was king of the world and deserved to live and be treated like one. John demolished the old farmhouse and built a new one. He spent more than $10,000 on brand new furniture. He also spent money on new clothes, including a $2,000 suit, which made him look like a mobster in a room full of farmers who hated wearing ties.

When he needed a truck to transport pigs from one barn to the other, John spent $200,000 to build a custom stainless steel vehicle with a state-of-the-art hydraulic system. He liked to show it off and everybody in the neighborhood came to see it. His neighbors, on the other hand, spent $2,000 on a used school bus that did the same trick. John was making these poor decisions because his ego was driving him. John's decision making was completely off. He was concerned about esteem, not financial safety.

John's father had set him up with the majority of shares in a newly formed corporation. Pig prices were exceptional for the first few years that John managed the company. When he looked at the farm's profits, he thought they were a result of his brilliant management, not a market upswing. Instead of using this excess capital to pay down loans, he spent it on his lifestyle. John drew $100,000 from the farm corporation in wages each year. So when the pig prices went south, John quickly ran out of money. John didn't know what it was like to fail. Bankruptcy was a harsh wake-up call that affected him and his father who was the co-signer on the farm.

"Farming With Family Ain't Always Easy!"

When John's grandfather Matthias had come to North America in the 1950s, he didn't care what kind of vehicle he drove or what kind of house he lived in; he was concerned only with stashing away cash and bought farms as cost-effectively as possible.

Had John managed the farm with the mentality of an immigrant who was grateful for the basics, the farm's profitability would have skyrocketed. But because a man with a third generation's perspective was managing the corporation, it failed miserably. People at the physiological level get out of bed in the morning because of a dire need to survive. However, people who are at the esteem level have wealth and feel they don't need to get out of bed.

The sense of entitlement can transform a once smooth-running farming operation into a business run by "teenage drama queens." Emotional behavior often takes over the most rational, well-run business and runs it into the ground quickly!

Hurt Feelings, Lost Profits

I recently worked with a family that was knee-deep in esteem issues. The third-generation son, Dave, kept shutting down the combine mid-day because his dad, Joe, wasn't talking to him 'nicely.' Stopping work was the last thing this farm needed especially since a major storm was moving in and the family could easily lose 100 acres of uninsured colored beans.

Meanwhile, the family spent much of the past year's record corn profits on new machinery, which was overkill for the size of farm that they ran. Their accountant, who was more preoccupied with taxation than farm management, had mistakenly given them the impression that they were in good financial shape. The bank also kept lending the farm money due to its asset base and that gave them a false sense of security.

"Farming With Family Ain't Always Easy!"

What Dave and Joe didn't realize was that although yields and corn prices had hit an all-time high the previous year, the farm had still lost $200,000. The best-case scenario for this year was similar. The family was on the edge of financial ruin and loosing an uninsured crop could quickly push them right over.

Dave and Joe needed to cut through all the drama and focus on saving this year's crop. They needed to put their egos aside and get down to work. If they didn't, the farm would be gone within five years.

They then needed to adapt a "we" instead of a "me, me, me" type of attitude. To do this, I got them to define both what was good for the individual and also for the farm. It got them focused. Once we did this, then they started pulling in the same direction.

Getting stuck on Maslow's esteem level can have a devastating impact on personal lives, too. A person who desires esteem is focused principally on himself and his own needs. He becomes a selfish narcissist. He tends to drink heavily and many times drinks alone. He thinks he's the only person in the world with problems, and no one can really understand how he feels. He feels that he is in a league of his own, and it's lonely at the top. He may have an extremely short temper and he may yell at his family frequently. He is likely unbearable to work with because he has no perception of anything around him; he lives in a world of me, me, me.

Getting stuck at the esteem level of Maslow's Hierarchy of Needs is one of agriculture's biggest unknown problems. As a mediator, I find that most of the clients who come to me with succession and interpersonal issues are stuck at this level.

The best way to lift the third-generation curse is to help self-entitled farmers change motivational levels. Some need to move

up; others need to move back down. For a younger third-generation farmer, give him $1,000, a ticket out of town, and a ride to the bus station. Tell him to work on a larger farm for at least two years before coming home. By doing this, you force your son to start at the bottom of the hierarchy.

It's important that your children learn what it's like to:
Work for someone else and get fired if he or she can't get out of bed in the morning.
Work for minimum wage and learn to balance his or her own finances on a limited budget.
Live without their family's reputation or money to fall back on.

In order to have full effect, kids must be sent at least 500 miles from home. Working for the neighbor while living rent-free at home defeats the purpose. Pushing your kids back to Level 1 makes them appreciate the opportunities they have when they do come home to farm.

Making a person live at Level 1 for a while works well for a younger farmer in his early 20s, but it's not really practical for a middle aged farmer who has a family. In that case, the best solution is to help everyone in the family move on to the top level of Maslow's hierarchy, self actualization.

Those at this level strive to realize their full potential, to be all they can be. They are driven by a higher cause and often live to solve a world's problem. They tend to be resourceful, self-sufficient, and independent. Farmers at the self-actualization level feel a strong desire to structure their farm's goals around a higher purpose.

Many successful family businesses engage in philanthropy. That means they give a portion of their profits to charity or another good cause. Philanthropy becomes a personal challenge for rich kids to squeeze extra profits to support their causes. It centers them. It makes them feel that they are on a mission, it gives them a new reason to get out of bed, and gets them on their way to becoming great managers.

"Farming With Family Ain't Always Easy!"

Unfortunately, too often Dad is at the social or esteem level and discourages sons from philanthropy because it takes time or money away from the business needs. However, if it's balanced, doing charity can improve all aspects of the farm. Here is an example of a self-actualized man who improved himself, his family relationships, and the farm all at the same time.

Evolving to the Top Level: Self-Actualization

Even though his father Bob and his brother Randy showed all the classic signs of being stuck at the esteem level, Ed spent his time attending farming conferences and coaching a local minor hockey team. Ed wanted to avoid the trap Randy had fallen into—one of low self-esteem, depression, and alcoholism—and teaching kids how to play hockey gave Ed a higher purpose. The rest of the family was critical of how much time Ed spent off the farm, especially since they were already down a man because Randy spent at least six weeks every year in rehab. The family thought Ed was just being lazy. What no one understood was that the time that Ed spent away from the farm coaching hockey kept him from needing rehab like Randy. Ed felt grateful for what he had. If he didn't spend that time doing charity, he would likely have been a self-centered addict like Randy. Ed was a happier man who pushed himself to "be all he could be," which resulted in great things for both the farm's profitability and his attitude.

Reaching the fifth level of Maslow's hierarchy improves relationships. People who are self-actualized tend to be more optimistic and pleasant to be around. The time they do spend on the farm is exponentially more productive. However, support is critical to their success. Without a family behind them, farmers aspiring to be better people can become downtrodden and depressed.

Reaching Level 5 is not an easy task, especially if the family is being torn apart by esteem issues. Asking a professional for advice will help ensure that you get on the right track and make

"Farming With Family Ain't Always Easy!"

the most of your time. The best practice is to have every shareholder and key employee see an executive coach. This person will help define personal and professional goals, and offer advice on how to achieve them. Meeting a coach helps you see the forest for the trees so you don't get lost in the woods. He or she is an objective person who will hold people accountable for their actions and inactions. Seeing a coach at least three times a year will help make sure things stay on the straight and narrow. In other words, an executive coach helps core members of the farm become the best they can be.

It's important for everyone to see the same executive coach on the same day and then to hold a family business meeting afterward. This family meeting serves as a place where the whole family can share goals, motivations, and values. Then the family can start planning how to support one another for the good of the business and each other. Spending $200 an hour to talk to a good executive coach might seem ridiculous to a family that has become successful by being frugal. But a small investment up-front can help avoid conflicts that can have a devastating impact on your profitability down the road.

John and Kenny Struggle for Time Off

John set a personal goal of attending more of his daughter's soccer games. Last year, he missed many of them because he was stuck looking after cows that were calving, even though his single brother Kenny could have taken over on game nights. Eventually John began to resent his brother for not pulling his weight. At the same time, Kenny felt like he could never get off the farm on a Saturday night to go on a date. They asked me to help them out. The two brothers started scheduling "calving watch" hours to support each other's dreams. This simple solution really improved their partnership and their quality of life.

Putting goals out in the open with an executive coach helps everyone understand motivations and allows family members to

"Farming With Family Ain't Always Easy!"

support each other. Individuals are happier when they feel like they are being heard and can work toward something they want, and the group is happier because everyone is working together for the good of the farm. Everyone has a hand in where the farm is going and how it is getting there. It transforms the culture of the farm from one of expecting to one of giving.

The third generation curse is a real conundrum. It's critical to pay attention to inner drivers and goals because they have a huge impact on the farm's bottom line.

Transforming a $4 million farm into a $40 million company requires a complete shift in thinking. Encouraging a "be all you can be" mindset will help everyone through this transition. Few operations overcome the third generation curse. The question is, will yours?

Chapter 4: Farming is Emotional

When I was in New Zealand, I went to a farm management competition where I talked to one of the judges about how he determined the winner. His answer was simple, yet surprising. His secret was that he talked to all the wives. I was taken aback by this response because I was really interested in production at that time and I thought he would have judged the competitors by measuring each farm's return-on-investment. But the judge explained that he knew who was going to be the better farmer by talking to each wife. In the end, he said, if a wife really wants the farm to succeed, it will. But if she doesn't care whether or not the farm succeeds, she's not going to kick her husband out of bed at five o' clock in the morning when the alarm goes off.

It's these little things that make a farm succeed. At first, I disagreed with the judge and thought he was being chauvinistic. But now I think he was right. It doesn't matter whether the spouse is male or female; and it doesn't matter whether they actually get dirt under their fingernails. What matters is the amount of emotional support they offer their spouse.

The first five years of marriage are absolutely critical in determining the amount of support a spouse will give to her partner and to the farm. Does he/she think of the farm as "his/her farm" or as "our farm?" This dynamic, along with the relationship he/she has with his/her in-laws, will have a big effect on whether the farm succeeds.

More often than not, when a couple gets married, the "in-laws" are still business partners with their son or daughter. Whether the newcomer becomes truly engaged in the family farm depends on how he or she is treated (or mistreated) by the in-laws. For example, if the husband's family is in constant conflict with their daughter-in-law and the issues between them don't get resolved, the daughter-in-law will eventually detach from the operation

"Farming With Family Ain't Always Easy!"

emotionally. Often the daughter-in-law will then encourage her spouse to invest less time on the farm and eventually seek off-farm employment. This has serious consequences on the viability and future of the operation.

As much as a person might try to avoid them, conflicts are going to happen. Whether they involve the business partners or family, smart farmers don't bury their heads in the sand and hope that the problems will just go away. Smart farmers put a system in place to deal with problems before they become crises and know exactly what to do when something comes up.

Once I interviewed a successful farmer who also shared a very large agribusiness with his brothers. He mentioned that twice a year, all three brothers, along with their wives, went to dinner at a quiet little restaurant 40 miles from their hometown. Their pastor was present as well, to facilitate the meeting.

Everyone would sit down to eat and to talk together about everything from work hours, to vacation time, to wages. They also discussed shared assets like housing and access to family vehicles. In other words, they proactively talked about all the issues that negatively affected the business and the family.

Although these meetings were sometimes tense, no one left until all of the issues were sorted out. This family learned to accept that conflicts were bound to happen in a partnership and developed a method to deal with them before they grew, bogged down the business, and tore the family apart. These meetings likely saved both the family and the farm. Before they came up with this system, the brothers were ready to split their partnership, but now they all get along. They even take holidays together!

It wasn't just the men who participated in these meetings. Whether or not they're officially business partners, it's important to include spousal opinions and insights when attempting to

"Farming With Family Ain't Always Easy!"

prevent conflicts. Designating a time and place for the sisters-in-law to address their pet peeves kept everyone engaged in the farm's success. It gave everyone a platform to express concerns in constructive not destructive ways, thus fixing problems or even pet peeves before they festered.

A family meeting shouldn't be all business. It should also carve out a place to talk about emotions. Farming is emotional, and our deepest feelings are powerful. It's critical that families accept the nature of each other's raw emotions and manage them before they profoundly impact the family business.

Brothers Divided

The priest called me in after he had to stop two brothers from killing each other at their father's funeral the day before.

They were devout Catholics who attended church regularly and they tried to convince everyone around them that their family was perfect. The priest, the brothers, and I sat in the father's empty house listening to the clock tick. The two boys simply weren't talking and they had no intention to start. They couldn't even look each other in the eye, and it was clear to me that either one of them could at any moment come across the table and pummel the other. Years of mutual hate and resentment had festered.

We were getting nowhere fast. I asked the priest to stay in the house and told the boys to put their boots on. They both looked at me, baffled, but they followed me outside into the cold. I led them behind the shed. When the one brother asked me what they were doing there, I said that if they weren't willing to sit down and sort out their differences like business partners, they might as well scrap like cavemen. You should have seen their heads turn when they heard that. And then they stood off.

"Farming With Family Ain't Always Easy!"

I told them that their dad was a great man, but he had his faults, just like everyone else. One of his faults was that he pitted his sons against one another in order to get what he wanted. The competition that had made them into exceptional men and had made the farm grow so quickly for the past 15 years also made them lousy business partners. I said that they could go ahead and fight for their daddy's love, but since they had laid him to rest the day before, fighting now wouldn't do them any good.

I swear that minute was the longest minute of my life. It was a bloody cold day and the wind howled around the shed. At last their fists went soft. It was a hell of a gamble that paid off.

Now that the boys were ready to listen to me, I tried to break down their situation. I told them that they could pay their lawyers to split this farm, but since it carried too much debt, doing so would forfeit their economies of scale and force them to take on an extra debt load that they wouldn't be able to manage during tough times. The bottom line was that they would both be broke in 10 years. I urged them to think about everything their dad and grandpa worked for….gone. All because they couldn't find a way to get along and work together.

I watched as one brother's eyes turned red, as if he were about to cry. The other brother's face was white with shock.

Finally, they started to realize that things had to change. If they didn't fix their relationship here and now, I warned them that the next 15 years of their life would be hell. It's true that their dad called all the shots and didn't teach them how to make decisions together, but now they had to pull together and learn to be a team. It was time for them to put aside the feelings of jealousy that their father had nurtured in them. I reminded them that they both professed to be good Christians, and now it was time to prove it. Either they forgive each other, or stop going to church. Period.

"Farming With Family Ain't Always Easy!"

I told the brothers that I was going to get the case of beer I had in the trunk of my car and wait inside where it was warm. They were welcome to join me only if they shook hands and agreed to solve their business issues like adults "It's you boys against the world from here on," I said.

They did polish off that case of beer together that day and a lot of their interpersonal problems got sorted out. They still have issues that they are working on, but at least they are going ahead and the farm is flourishing. Sometimes it takes a breakthrough moment to deal with the issues of the past to really make the future work. More importantly, they recognized the need to not fight for control and to use a third party to help them make decisions together.

Siblings can farm together. They just need to set aside childhood issues and learn to make decisions together as mature adults.

Turf Wars

Andrew was a bachelor until he was 28. Even though he lived in a house down the road from his parents, his mother still cooked and cleaned for him regularly. He didn't even own a frying pan, until his wedding shower.

When Andrew married, his mother loved her new daughter-in-law to bits and the two quickly became best friends. But six months later it was a completely different story and the "in-laws" were now the "out-laws." Sometimes another person walking onto the farm throws the family dynamics off balance. The women became jealous of each other and struggled to find their new place in Andrew's life. They were having a turf war. Essentially, two women loved Andrew in different ways, and he didn't know what to do.

It's the deep emotional issues—like jealousy—that can hit you like a frying pan across the back of your head and ruin your family

"Farming With Family Ain't Always Easy!"

business. Molehills become mountains overnight, and if you don't have a plan in place for how to deal with them, you may lose it all.

It's important to take the time to figure out what is behind the feelings. Many newlywed farming couples are living their parents' dream. These parents worked hard their entire lives to provide an opportunity for the next generation to farm more land and to enjoy a higher standard of living than they had. If the young couple isn't careful, they can be perceived as ungrateful.

For instance, a newlywed couple moved back to the groom's home farm into a house owned by his parents. After having their first child, the bride experienced post-partum depression and started to miss her former lifestyle of living in the city. As a result, problems in the marriage arose.

Looking for a way to increase her happiness on the farm, the wife decided she'd like to buy a horse. Immediately, her in-laws shot down the idea. They didn't want any of their valuable cropland being run as pasture. Their decision left the new wife feeling trapped and unimportant in the farm's decision-making.

Shortly thereafter, the groom's parents went on holiday and when they returned home they passed by a horse standing in a pasture field that had only recently been planted with corn. The parents were shocked. It was the first time their son had gone against their word and they were furious.

When I met with this family, I explained to them that it was necessary for the son to over ride his parents' decision. He wasn't acting out to be rebellious; he was trying to keep his family together.

Some disagreement between parents and their young adult children is actually a good sign for the business. It shows that the next generation is figuring out how to do things on their own, even if it's different from the way things used to be done. It may take quite a while to adjust to the idea that your son has his own methods, but it a necessary step of maturity. If your son doesn't disagree with you at some critical point in the farm's history, he will never be fit to become the farm's CEO someday.

It's Either Me or Her

Sabrina and Matt had been married for only 18 months when Sabrina packed her bags and threatened to move back to Iowa. She loved her husband, but she didn't feel welcome on her husband's family farm. The trouble had started a year earlier when a feed salesman came to speak to Matt's father, Norm, about the animals. Sabrina had just finished her chores and joined in the conversation. Because she had a master's degree in nutrition, she posed some good questions to the nutritionist. Soon the conversation went over Norm's head. Norm felt that Sabrina had pushed him out of the conversation, and their relationship changed instantly. Within that moment, Norm thought that Sabrina had gone from being the ideal daughter-in-law to the witch that had to go. Deep down, Norm was afraid that Sabrina was going to start bossing him around. He was only 55 years old and wasn't ready to give up control. "It's either me or her," he said.

Narcissism is a term used to describe people who are extremely self-centered and oblivious to the needs and feelings of others. When it comes to farm succession, narcissism is one of the biggest threats to an operation's continued success.

Few people understand that for some men, the farm is the center of his identity. The farm is who he is. It is his pride and joy. If there is even an inkling that the farm is being taken over, he may get very defensive. He has spent his entire life building the business, and he is used to having people follow his instructions and trust his leadership.

"Farming With Family Ain't Always Easy!"

Norm was surprised to realize that when Sabrina got involved in 'his business,' he felt as if someone had come into his house and started kissing his wife. To watch as someone else took the lead with a salesmen felt like a huge betrayal to Norm, one similar to adultery. He felt that Sabrina had somehow taken what was his and because of that she couldn't be trusted any more. No longer feeling he could have Sabrina on his farm, Norm fired her.

Sabrina was devastated. She had grown up on one of the largest swine operations in her hometown. She lived and breathed hog farming, was extremely skilled and worked very hard. She loved her husband, but she loved farming more.

Matt continued to work 15-hour days on the farm and barely saw his wife. This was definitely not the marriage either of them had signed up for. Sabrina became homesick and depressed, and even thought about suicide.

Norm wasn't open to mediation. He didn't care about Sabrina or Matt's feelings. He only cared about his own insecurities and his need to be in control.

Norm was so wrapped up in being in charge that he was stunned when Matt dropped everything to follow his wife back to her family farm. Finding farmhands to complete Matt's share of the chores caused Norm nothing but headaches. He was forced to sell the sows within 18 months, leaving him with no farm and no family. Dad's infatuation with his own ego left nobody the winner.

This story shows just how powerful emotions can be. Norm, an experienced and mature man, felt so threatened when someone else seemed to know more than he did about hog husbandry, he took drastic action. In other words, his raw emotions caused him to make irrational decisions, like firing his daughter-in-law who could have been a huge asset to the operation. This kind of thing happens all too often.

"Farming With Family Ain't Always Easy!"

Along with the fear of losing control of the farm, the fear of divorce is a quiet menace to farm succession and overall farm business management. The stress of managing a business and working with in-laws, combined with a more tolerant attitude toward divorce in the younger generation means that the rate of farm divorce is skyrocketing. When huge assets like farms are involved, divorce has a big impact on the rural economy. Divorce could cause more farms to become insolvent in the next decade than the total number that failed over the past century.

The parents are often the ones who take steps to protect the farm from the financial impact of a potential divorce. In the past, parents would prepare for a battle as soon as they thought they saw a "dark side" to their new daughter-in-law. Some parents even go so far as to ask their daughter-in-law to sign a pre- or postnuptial agreement, sometimes five years after the wedding! Other parents delay succeeding the farm to their married children because they fear divorce. Ironically, these actions often cause divorces, not prevent them.

Pre-nuptial agreements can be toxic to farm success. The person required to sign one may feel excluded from the success of the farm and detach emotionally from it. If she has no skin in the game, she won't be as driven to help the farm succeed because she knows that someday she might be shoved out. The rest of the family may always treat her as an outsider. Without financial security, she is more likely to seek off-farm employment because she has to look out for herself. It will always seem like her husband's farm, not our farm.

Family support is crucial to farm success so it makes sense to think about how to reduce the probability of divorce and increase the amount of quality time a husband and wife can spend together. Everyone has a role to play. Younger spouses and their parents or in-laws need to take some responsibility for making the relationship work, even through the rough patches.

"Farming With Family Ain't Always Easy!"

Getting along with everyone on the farm makes good business sense. Forcing anyone to sign a prenuptial agreement is bound to start the relationship off on the wrong foot, and no matter how air-tight you think the legal agreement might be, it might not be worth the paper it's written on. On the other hand, staying on good terms may convince a divorcing spouse not to demand everything he or she is legally entitled to because she is still in love with the family. However, if the in-laws are part of the problem, and there is a lot of shared animosity and bitterness, a spouse may take as much as he or she can out of anger and resentment. It's just smart to play nice!

Every family needs to recognize that a new bride's (or groom's) emotional involvement in the farm will ultimately determine the farm's long-term success.

When a new person comes into the family, weird things happen. People who are typically rational, kind, and down-to-earth may suddenly make erratic decisions due to deep-seeded fears that they themselves might not know about. It's a very good idea to discuss these things with an outsider so that these feelings can stay in check. You don't want to be the one who causes your son's or daughter's divorce. Remember, it's not what you say, but how you say it. It's important that your family has a time and place to deal with problems before they fester and grow. If you don't acknowledge people's feelings, then any attempts at a partnership will eventually fail!

Farming with family ain't always easy. But addressing these issues head-on will help resolve the majority of the problems you encounter before they cause damage.

"Farming With Family Ain't Always Easy!"

Chapter 5: Changing How You Manage Change

"Haven't I done anything right?" Hank screamed at me.

Hank was stuck in his ways. He had spent his entire life working towards a single goal: pay off all his debts and make his dairy farm incredibly profitable. With a lot of hard work and sacrifice, he had achieved that goal in his sixties. He thought that his son would be grateful to have such a nice farm to take over, but things didn't look like they were going to turn out that way.

Hank's son Derek had graduated from agriculture college and had spewed out thousands of ideas over the past three years. It was as if Derek couldn't help but offer a new million-dollar idea every day. The problem was that most of his ideas would actually cost a million dollars but would never return the investment.

The year after Derek returned home from college, he went behind his father's back to get a pre-approved loan for a major barn expansion. When Hank got the call from the bank regarding this plan, he was furious. Needless to say, the expansion didn't happen. When Hank put his foot down, Derek's attitude toward his Dad changed. He criticized his father's every move. The two men went from being the best of friends to worst of enemies almost overnight. The accountant called me in to mediate the crisis, and I arrived at the farm just as Derek was removing his belongings from the "hired man's" house with a plane ticket in his hand.

The problem wasn't the barn expansion plan; it was that neither Derek nor Hank had a system in place to deal with change. Derek didn't know how to bring up new ideas so his father would listen, and Hank didn't know how to be open to the good ones, or to challenge the bad ones without running Derek down.

"Farming With Family Ain't Always Easy!"

I asked Hank, "Are you going to define change or is it going to define you?" Like it or not, things were about to change. Either Hank would have to learn to take input from his son, or learn to live and work without him. Without an heir, he would have to sell the farm and change his lifestyle completely. Both men needed to transform how they viewed change and how they dealt with it.

Change is difficult, and it's a tough topic to discuss. That's why facilitated monthly family business meetings that focus on managing change successfully are a good idea. Here is how I structure the discussion:

Step 1: Brainstorm: I tell every family member to come to the table prepared to present one simple idea for change. They have to think through their idea, not to just blurt out the first thought that comes to mind. The proposed change can't cost more than 1 per cent of the farm's assets, and must pay the farm back in an appropriate amount of time. The simpler the change and the higher the return, the better.

Step 2: Evaluate the Idea: Once all of the proposals are on the table, the family and I discuss each idea together. I help them weigh the pros and cons, and make sure each person has enough time to express his or her opinion. It's critical that everyone participates at this stage. If a family member is reluctant to speak, I encourage them and I remind them that this is the time and place for different perspectives.

If the family is having trouble discussing the ideas in productive ways, as the meeting facilitator, I can go into my toolbox and introduce more complex decision-making tools (ex. De Bono's Six Hats). This is just one the ways I can help a family look at issues from a different viewpoint and communicate with each other more effectively.

We start small. Learning how to evaluate simple ideas can teach everyone how to evaluate bigger strategic problems down the

"Farming With Family Ain't Always Easy!"

road. Once the technique is mastered, no matter what comes up, the family will have a process to follow to ensure that everyone has a say.

Step 3: Make a Decision: Once everyone has had a chance to say what they think about each idea, it's time to make a decision. Making a decision is a process in itself. Here are the three steps I encourage my clients to follow:

Decide on how to decide. Will it be by consensus, by simple majority, or done by the person in charge?
Put a timeline on the decision. When will the final decision be made? Sometimes it's best to delay making certain decisions to another meeting in order to give people time to do more research, or just more time to think about it. But, at some point, a decision has to be made. Giving the process a timeline prevents procrastination.

Make sure that the decision making process is objective and civil. Having a facilitator present to make sure one party isn't a "bully" is key. Decisions shouldn't be made by the loudest voice or the person who speaks most frequently.

Step 4: Follow Through: It's easy to discuss an idea, but it can be hard to decide how good it is. It's even harder to make sure the decision gets implemented. Implementation of a change is actually one of the most difficult challenges a family business can face. A facilitator can help hold family members accountable for doing what they say they will do, which means no one in the family has to act as an enforcer. It takes the pressure off family members and really diffuses tensions.

It's one thing to come up with ideas for improvements, but it's another for everyone within the family to buy into those changes and actually make them a reality. The following story is an example of what can happen when a family doesn't work together to discuss new ideas and implement change.

"Farming With Family Ain't Always Easy!"

There are Many Ways to Milk a Cow

Ken and his sons owned and operated a family dairy operation. One day, the sons decided to change the milking procedures to incorporate a suggestion from a veterinarian. Ken was made aware of the new procedure but nonetheless continued to milk the cows his way. In his mind nobody was going to tell him how to milk his cows. Not surprisingly, a pattern developed. Every few days after Ken did the milking, the number of mastitis cases spiked (when cows get sick) because Dad refused to conform to the farm's new milking procedures.

There are many ways to milk a cow. It doesn't matter how you milk them; what matters is that everyone milks the same cows in the same way. The same principle is true for farm management in general. There are many ways to run a farm, but everyone has to follow the same methods to succeed.

Getting everyone to agree on a standard milking procedure results in more milk in the tank and less milk dumped on the floor.

Not everyone in a family business is going to agree with every decision made. But refusing to "go along with the team" even though the decision was reached fairly creates a culture of conflict and gives the holdout a reputation of being stubborn and inflexible. Being a stick-in-the-mud creates a dysfunctional business environment and strains relationships.

Of course, there has to be an opportunity to discuss the pros and cons of a suggestion before it becomes a decision. But once a decision is made, you've got to do your best to follow through, regardless of your reservations. There is no "I" in team. Putting

your team's decisions before your own ego will make your farm successful in the long run. How well people implement ideas, not the ideas themselves, will determine whether your farm will prosper. Don't be self-centered. Be a team player.

"Farming With Family Ain't Always Easy!"

Step 5: Learn from Mistakes: Learning from mistakes is the most important part of the family decision-making process. Most families never discuss mistakes unless it's in a vindictive tone and during a family argument about an unrelated matter. As a result, the organization never learns and improves. It's one of agriculture's greatest failures.

In reality, not everything works. Ask yourself the following questions to figure out what went well and what could have been done better:

1. Did the decision succeed as projected?
2. What information did we not have at the time that would have improved the probability of success?
3. How would we make the decision differently next time?
4. Did our team have trouble implementing the idea?
5. How can we make sure that we don't make the same mistakes twice?

It is very important that everyone in the family participates in this process as a group. Just like a basketball team, try to instill the attitude that we win together and lose together. Pointing fingers will only stall future success. If this process is done well, you will not only be teaching the next generation how to be the most knowledgeable farmers, but also how to be wiser decision makers.

Beyond the Steps...

It usually takes toddlers five years to learn table manners. It takes even longer than that to learn how to make decisions at the table

together. But once a family has figured out how to make small decisions together, it can use the same tools to discuss and decide on larger strategic issues.

"Farming With Family Ain't Always Easy!"

I think changing how a family deals with change are the most critical skills a family can learn. Change is going to happen whether you're ready for it or not. Without the ability to address change in a proactive way, the majority of changes that affect your family will have negative consequences. Don't be afraid to start small. Remember, one of the reasons the Titanic sank was because it couldn't change course at full speed. Starting small and working your way towards bigger, more significant, and more expensive changes will give you the confidence to handle any situation. Work hard now to develop your skills to discuss and manage change so that you have the ability to deal with change when big events arise. Your farm, and your family, will thank you.

Chapter 6: Pulling in the Same Direction

Former United States President John F. Kennedy told the world that he wanted to "put a man on the moon in 10 years."

Who could have predicted that such a simple statement would have inspired so many people and change the course of history? JFK was an expert at uniting people, at motivating them to push themselves beyond their own limits. He understood that a simple and clear message could steer millions and allow them to achieve what seemed impossible. His message was so powerful that it continued to resonate after his death—and his mission was accomplished! It's time to take a page from Kennedy's book and use simple messaging to pull your family together and move your business forward.

Far too often families have no vision of what the farm—or their lives—will look like in a decade. Without some planning and an agreement on the final destination, everyone will end up in a place they don't want to be.

Imagine a father-and-son team embarking on a road trip in an old, beat-up truck. The son wants to go skiing in Utah; the father wants to enjoy the sun in Florida. They start at the Canada-U.S. border. The father starts driving south while the son naps. The son wakes up a few hours later and offers to drive. When he takes the wheel, he changes courses starts driving west. They never talk to each other. One just keeps driving south, and the other keeps driving west. At the end of the week, they look up and realize that they're out of money, out of gas, and stuck in a snowstorm in Muskogee, Oklahoma.

If a family doesn't take the time to talk about and agree on a precise end destination, its members will always end up miserable, in a spot where no one wants to be. Had the father and son in the example above just talked it out, they could have

"Farming With Family Ain't Always Easy!"

compromised on a place they both liked: Nashville for instance. The father could have enjoyed himself at the Grand Ole Opry and the son could have had a good time out on the town. They could have been there in 10 hours, instead of spending a frustrating week stuck in the truck in the middle of a snowstorm.

Sometimes a family can agree on a final destination in five minutes. Sometimes it takes quite a bit longer. Either way, it's an important investment of valuable time because it not only lays a clear path for your business, but can also help you avoid most family conflicts.

This is where a business plan can help. A business plan's purpose isn't to get money from the bank. It's to put money in the bank!

A business plan isn't just facts and figures outlining projected expenses and profit. It spells out the family member's expectations.

Too many parent-and-child teams disagree over work/life balance. Most often, Dad spends his life in the barn, while the son wants to spend more time with his wife and kids.

Both the father and the son have good points. Too little work means you can't afford to put food on your table or keep a roof over your head. Too much work means stress on your marriage, potential divorce, and even losing your home altogether. Work/life balance is complicated. There is no easy or generic solution, but talking about what each person wants for himself and expects of the other, and spelling it out in a business plan, will go a long way toward avoiding conflict.

Here's an example of a family at its wit's end because they didn't talk to each other about balancing their responsibilities to the farm and the family.

"Farming With Family Ain't Always Easy!"

Growing at Any Cost

Martha and her son Eric owned a 200 cow dairy, a 5,000 head hog finishing operation and ran over 2,000 acres of land. Martha worked hard, and she expected everyone else to work like she did. In the course of one year, she had fired one hand, one had quit, and her husband had died of cancer. Meanwhile, the farm was going deeper and deeper into debt due to low hog prices and challenges around dairy production. Instead of hiring replacement labor, Martha decided that she and Eric would simply work more hours. Eric reluctantly went along with the plan.

Hog prices eventually went back up and the dairy's production challenges were finally resolved. The long hours Eric had invested in working on the farm had paid off. Still, Eric's wife Emily and their two young children barely saw him, except for a few brief moments when Emily delivered meals to him in the barn. Emily loved her husband dearly, but Eric's long hours were starting to wear on their marriage, and she desperately wanted to find time for them to be together. She was only asking for Eric to take Sunday afternoons off so they could get away from the farm and do things together like a normal family. Now that they could afford it, Emily started to insist that they hire a couple of men to do some of Eric's work.

Martha thought that Emily was being silly. Martha was happy that the farm was finally turning a profit and she wanted to invest the money into more land, not labor. She had a grand vision for the business and felt that the long hours Eric spent working were perfectly reasonable for any ambitious farmer. After all, she thought, farming was a seven-day-a-week kind of job.

But Emily had had enough. She left a note on the kitchen door saying that she and the children had gone to her mother's, and that she was going to file for divorce unless an extra man was hired by the end of the month.

"Farming With Family Ain't Always Easy!"

The family called me in for help. You should have seen Martha's look of horror when I made her realize that if Emily filed for divorce, Emily would be entitled to half the equity of her farming empire, placing the family in a precarious financial situation from which they could never recover. Thirty seconds later I watched her cry as she also realized that her grandson would grow up in the city five hours away and more than likely never become a farmer like she had.

Martha and her son Eric had different visions for their lives. Martha was obsessed with maximizing net profit and was willing to do whatever it took to achieve it. Eric and his wife wanted a more balanced life even if it meant earning less. Emily should never have had to issue an ultimatum to get what she wanted, especially when her expectations were reasonable. The family needed a way to define an ideal state for both the business and the family.

The root of this conflict was that everyone had a different vision of a successful farm and a successful family life. Keeping their expectations secret until the very end almost caused the family and the farm to implode. In order for a business to succeed, everyone has to buy into the same plan. If they don't, everyone works according to his or her own agenda and pulls the farm in different directions.

Drafting a Business Plan

The first step to building a business plan has nothing to do with writing words on paper. First, every family member has to think carefully about how they want their personal lives to look both now and 10 years into the future. They should ask themselves what kind of lifestyle they want, and what amount of work they would have to commit to in order to generate enough money to support it. Next, they must ask themselves what kind of business

"Farming With Family Ain't Always Easy!"

they want to pass on to their children, and what personal sacrifices would be necessary to make it happen.

Not every family needs a 5,000 acre farm to be happy or satisfy their lifestyle. Bigger isn't always better. That is why it is so critical to discuss personal goals prior to business goals.

Now it's time to write things down. Each person should turn his or her dream life into a one-page personal plan that describes how he/she wants life to be different in the future. They should also include a "bucket list" of personal goals they want to achieve, such as travelling to Egypt to see the pyramids or learning how to ride a motorcycle. Make sure that each plan considers how goals may change after major life events occur. For instance, a 22-year-old bachelor farm boy may be willing to work 18-hour days now, but he may want more time off when he becomes a 29-year-old man with three kids. Once everyone has written down and discussed their personal goals, it's time for the family to formulate a common business plan.

JFK described his vision of NASA's future in one line. What one liner will get everyone in your family striving toward the same goals?

A strategic business plan should address five simple questions:
Vision: What will the farm look like in 10 years?

Mission: What makes your approach to farming different from your neighbor's?

Core Values: What makes your operation different from your neighbor's?

Strategies: What are your five biggest competitive advantages and your five greatest weaknesses that you want to turn into strengths?

"Farming With Family Ain't Always Easy!"

Strategic Objectives: What major purchases and changes do you plan to make over the next five years? Consider equipment, buildings, land, etc.

A business plan shouldn't be a fancy document created to please a bank or other investors. It should be a simple one-page plan of action specific to the needs of your farm and the people on it. Very few farms have written a strategic plan over the past 40 years, and those that have, tend to store them in a filing cabinet never to be thought of again. A good strategic plan outlines your destination, a route that details how to get there, and a way to navigate detours so that you can get back on track without losing your cool.

Once written, your plan should be everywhere—at the front gates, above the toilet—any place you and your farm employees can see it every day. If you keep it in a filing cabinet, the plan won't work. Putting your plan out in the open is a key driver towards success.

Certain tactics, such as arranging to buy a farm by having the neighbor take back the mortgage might be kept more secretive. But the "big picture" should be a simple plan everyone knows.

Part of keeping your plan out in the open means that you—and everybody else— should be talking about it all the time. A lot of families like to guard their business plan as if it were a military secret. It's silly because no matter how hard you may try, your plan to grow is obvious to your neighbors. If you keep it under lock and key, the chances are that you'll forget about it yourself, and so will your employees and the rest of your family. Everyone has to know what the plan is if it's going to happen.

Had NASA kept President Kennedy's strategy a secret, the United States may never have sent a man to the moon.

"Farming With Family Ain't Always Easy!"

Here's a simple example of a family that benefited from defining clear goals:

I once worked with a family who ran a cash crop operation. They had no clear goal when it came to crop production targets, and their profits suffered as a result. After they developed a clear plan, one of their core strategies was to "increase income by 25 per cent by more closely monitoring crop markets and hedging risks." Had that one line been lost in the back of a filing cabinet, everyone would have forgotten it within a week, and probably nothing would have been implemented. On many busy farms like this one, strategic initiatives soon fall by the wayside in favor of daily routines and dealing with unexpected crises. But because the family had their business plan out in the open, everyone couldn't help but read it. Over the course of two years, the family significantly changed how it managed the operation's crop marketing. This meant the strategy was actually implemented and they achieved their goal.

A business plan is the easiest way to get everyone focused on what matters. When you go on a long road trip to somewhere you haven't been before, you don't just look at the map for a few minutes and throw it into the glove box. No, you keep it on the seat next to you and you look at it throughout the trip. You check off when you achieve milestones and use it as a guide to get back on track when you hit detours.

Once everyone starts pulling in the same strategic direction, everything else is like water running downhill.

"Farming With Family Ain't Always Easy!"

Chapter 7: Continuous Improvement

North American business culture thrives on blaming someone else when things go wrong. As a result, not only do people hide their weaknesses from each other, but they also spend an enormous amount of time and energy trying to convince the rest of the world that they are perfect. What would happen if we stopped pretending to be perfect? What would happen if we identified our greatest weaknesses and worked together to fix them?

The Japanese car manufacturing industry embraced Edward Deming's philosophy of continuous improvement. Thanks to his belief that exposing imperfections will help a business improve, Toyota built better quality cars more quickly and more cheaply than anyone else. It's time for North American family businesses to adopt these ideas and reap the benefits for themselves. We need to proactively fix mistakes!

It makes sense for a family to stop avoiding mistakes and to start seeing them as opportunities to improve. But facing failure requires a major shift in the way we think about 'failure' and our relationship to it. If not done tactfully, seeking out your own and other people's mistakes can end up hurting people's feelings. That's why it's so important to start by focusing on an issue that is small and impersonal, like production issues, and gradually move on to more strategic and interpersonal issues.

A meeting chairman can keep the conversation productive and help you look at your problems in a variety of ways. One of the problem solving tools I introduce to families is called *Layman's Six Sigma*.

I always tell folks to think of *Layman's Six Sigma* as a target at a shooting range. The bull's-eye represents the ideal scenario, and several circles around it to make up the rest of the target. The idea is to take any measurable element of your farm's operation,

"Farming With Family Ain't Always Easy!"

called a metric, and see how close it is to the ideal situation. Are you hitting the bull's-eye? If not, how far away from it are you? And, most importantly, how will you correct your sights so you can hit it next time?

There's Nothing Wrong with the Cows

I once worked with clients who had a reputation for running one of the best-managed dairy farms in Elgin County. From the outside, it looked as though there wasn't a blade of grass out of place. The family took great pride in seeming perfect.

The truth was that the three brothers were constantly bickering to the point that they were ready to split the operation. After two failed attempts at solving the conflict with other mediators, they called me in to help.

The family was surprised when I came right out and said, "What are your biggest weaknesses?" No one had asked them that before, and they had begun to believe their own stories that they were perfect. It took me three hours to figure out that the real source of the conflict was that no one knew why the cows weren't getting pregnant. That day I helped them set some reasonable goals, including a target pregnancy of 20%.

Over the next 6 months, I helped everyone change the way they looked at and dealt with conflict. Instead of falling back into the habit of blaming someone else for a problem on the farm, I encouraged them to see it as a common issue that they needed to work together to solve. Taking blame out of the equation meant each person had more energy to spend on improving the way the farm worked. Once I taught the family how to see problems differently, it was time to work with the numbers. Each month I asked the family what the actual pregnancy rate was, and then compared it to the 'bull's-eye' rate of 20%. If it wasn't on target, I asked the family why, and we started problem solving together.

"Farming With Family Ain't Always Easy!"

As it turned out, there was nothing wrong with the cows. The problem was that the family wasn't communicating. On busy days, each person thought someone else was watching the cows for signs of heat. No one made notes, so the cow breeder simply thought that there were no cows to breed.

Once they realized that it was their communication habits that were letting them down, it was time to find out what that was costing them. Every month we compared the target metric with the actual metric for that month. In this example, the target metric was a 20% pregnancy rate for first time breeding, and the current metric was 14%. Next we made a rough estimate of how much a 6% difference meant in terms of profit. For that 300-cow herd, the difference was about $115,000 per year. Seeing the numbers on paper motivated everyone to change their behavior. It got everyone focused on problem solving.

This was a "get it done" type of family who thought "communication" was a word that hippies used. As soon as they realized that they could save $115,000 by changing the way they communicated, things clicked in. It wasn't wishy-washy stuff to them anymore. It had a serious impact on the farm's profitability.

Once they realized it was ok to seek out imperfections in order to try to improve them, they started farming smarter and stopped wasting money. Seeing the numbers in black and white really motivated the whole family to change how they faced problems together. Instead of blaming each other, they stuck together as a team to make important decisions. As a result of this cultural change, the three brothers are now building a $2,000,000 barn expansion.

A family can keep track of more than one metric at a time. Once it has determined where is now compared to where it wants to be, I post both numbers on a "scoreboard" at key traffic points where family and non-family members can see them. For a dairy farm, I like to post a scoreboard in the shop, by the milk tank, and

"Farming With Family Ain't Always Easy!"

in the farm office. Seeing them every day helps everyone focus on working together to turn the farm's weaknesses into strengths.

Comparing current metrics to ideal metrics won't fix everything, but it will help people stop pointing fingers at one another and start everyone working together to solve common problems. Eventually the goal is to accept that "we aren't perfect but we have the tools to improve." Once a family gets used to working together toward a common goal, it can tackle just about any issue, from human resources to major strategic changes.

If it worked for them, then it can work for you.

Chapter 8: Next Steps: The Rock, Paper, Scissors Method

After reading this book, I hope that you've realized that the way your family makes decisions affects your farm's profitability more than the markets and weather together.

Talking is good, but only action creates success. Sometimes it's difficult to know where to begin. I encourage you to start by making three simple changes:

1. Get everyone to agree to a one-page strategy and post it everywhere.

2. Create a list of your top 10 weaknesses and work on them together.

3. Set up a monthly management meeting, and use a third party facilitator to help your family improve how it works together.

I like to call it the ROCK, PAPER, SCISSORS method.

Rock- "Take a Stone Out of Your Shoe"

Every farmer has enough common sense to sit down to take a stone out of his shoe before that stone injures his foot. However, most farm families don't see the value in creating a time or place to sit down to discuss small issues before they fester and become big problems.

A monthly business meeting creates a defined space where everyone can sit down and shake all the figurative rocks out of their shoes. A facilitator can help everyone present their issues and work through them together in a proactive way.

"Farming With Family Ain't Always Easy!"

In addition to a monthly meeting with the partners, I recommend a quarterly meeting that includes the partners' spouses. These meetings should focus on issues that affect the whole family, from buying land to setting wages.

Paper- "One Page Strategic Plan"

"Paper" means creating a one-page business plan that outlines where the farm is going and how it is going to get there. Post the plan everywhere so that everyone grasps what he or she has to do every day to achieve the farm's long-term strategic vision. It gets everyone pulling in the same direction.

Scissors- "Set Goals Together & Cut the Fat"

"Scissors" means setting bold, metric-driven goals and trimming the fat until your organization achieves them.

When it comes to measurable goals, knowing where you are compared to where you want to be is essential for success. Keeping the targets out in the open reminds everyone that there is still work to be done. Assessing the farm's progress every month (good, bad, or ugly) motivates everyone to work together to find solutions. Everyone is united in the quest to get rid of ineffective procedures unhelpful attitudes, or poor communication in order to make the farm as efficient as possible.

"Farming With Family Ain't Always Easy!"

Conclusion

I believe that families can and should work together.

The problems we have today is in the way we make decisions together. If these problems are fixed it will both improve the farm succession experience and also how siblings to take on the world together thereafter.

In this book, I've discussed three big concepts:

Motivation: What drives us to get out of bed in the morning?
Fears: What behavior causes families to go off track?
Business Processes: What things can you do to stay on track?

I've made some suggestions about how to improve your business processes, but it's up to you to take them and apply them to your own situation. Regardless of farm size, evolving how your family makes decisions together will give your business a competitive edge and reduce frustrations.

Open and ongoing communication among all the stakeholders is essential to getting things done. That's why I highly recommend that your family hold business meetings with a facilitator or executive coach on a monthly or at least a quarterly basis. He or she can get everyone talking in a productive and respectful way, keep everyone focused on what really matters, and suggest strategies to overcome even the most difficult business and personal conflicts.

Developing decision-making procedures may seem nerdy and formal, but spending the time to set out how your family makes decisions will improve the quality of the decision you make and save you loads of time and money in the long run. It may even save your marriage!

"Farming With Family Ain't Always Easy!"

Once the process is in place, every family will have a roadmap to tackle even the toughest issues, like farm succession. No matter what life and business may throw your way, you'll have the tools you need to address problems and make positive, proactive decisions that will improve profitability and keep your family pulling in the same direction.

Don't wait until the bank starts calling and your spouse has one foot out the door. The key is to start somewhere, and to start now.

I'll say it again. Farming with family ain't always easy. There will always be those days when you want to punch your siblings or discipline your grown children the way you did 30 years ago. However, if you can eliminate most of your frustration by reengineering how your family makes decisions together, you'll be able to handle all that comes with the job.

What will you do today to make sure your family's name is on the mail box 100 years from now?

"Farming With Family Ain't Always Easy!"

Acknowledgements

I want to thank my editors:

Caitlin Renneson
Courtney Denard
Jeremy "Hillbilly" Surrette

My success is thanks to the moral support of the following people:

Dave Ireland, Dr. Rob Bell, Dr. Don Jonovic, Dr. Wayne Shewfelt, Dr. Scott Westlake, Mel Luymes, Karen Bilger, Jan Broeders, Brad Dent, Russel Hurst, Rodney Ireland, Matthew Cole, Carm Hamilton, Rolf Frischknecht,
Ed Tollenaar, Elliot Faust, Stew Slater, Greg Insley, Greg Shirk, Peter McSherry, Chad Burley, Christine Schoonderwoerd, Jamie Beaumont, Fred & Henry Koskamp.

Words can't thank you enough for your genuine friendships.

Chapter Summaries

Chapter 1: Gaining the Competitive Edge

A farm's business culture is rarely considered, but it affects farm profit more than the markets and weather combined.

The more effectively a family sets common goals and works together to achieve them, the more profitable a farm will be.

Farming is a competition with your neighbors for land based on efficiency. Improving the quality of your farm's decision making/execution will directly impact your farm's efficiency and long term growth.

Chapter 2: The Decade of Dysfunction

The cause of farm succession problems isn't the transfer of assets. It's the emotional issues created by a decade of a frustrated family trying to work together.

Transition from a culture of "me" to "we" is difficult for many farmers, especially if they are used to running the farm their way. Being open to new ideas and gradually letting go of control will help smooth tensions between the generations.

Spend time teaching the next generation what it needs to know about farming. Don't assume your children have automatically learned how to run a farm business.

Chapter 3: The Third Generation Curse

Learning what motivates people can help you maximize a person's contribution to the farm.

"Farming With Family Ain't Always Easy!"

Help your children keep perspective and appreciate what they have by sending them away to work a year. They need to starve before you can grow.

Challenge everyone to "be all they can be." Encourage them to engage in philanthropy. Focusing some energy on a greater cause makes people more efficient and pleasant to work with.

Chapter 4: Farming is Emotional

Regardless of daily involvement, a spouse's interest in the farm will greatly influence the farm's long-term success. In-laws should take special care to make the spouse feel included and respected.

Children are going to have different opinions from their parents. (Genesis 2:22)

Take a proactive approach to problem solving. Create a time and place where the whole family can present and discuss problems. Use a facilitator to make sure these meetings are constructive, not destructive.

Chapter 5: Changing How You Manage Change

Change is difficult, but it's bound to happen. Try to stay flexible and manage change proactively.

Develop an objective process for proactively discussing and evaluating new ideas.

Once a decision is made, do your best to follow through. Have a method to hold everyone accountable for his or her actions.

Practice making small decisions together as a family as soon as possible so you are comfortable making big ones someday.

"Farming With Family Ain't Always Easy!"

Chapter 6: Pulling in the Same Direction

Define your family's shared vision for the farm in a single sentence.

Identify personal goals and work them into the farm's long-term plan.

Create a one-page business plan and post it on the kitchen fridge for all to see.

Chapter 7: Continuous Improvement

Resist the temptation to brag about your strengths. Identify your weaknesses and become an expert at turning your imperfections into strategic strengths.

Choose a few metrics and compare where they are now to where you want them to be. Where appropriate, calculate the cost of being off the mark to motivate people to change.

Post scoreboards of key business metrics throughout the farm. Although a bit embarrassing, posting failures will focus you on changing behavior and achieving success.

Chapter 8 Next Steps: The Rock, Paper, Scissors Method

Rock- Have a time and place to shake out "pet peeves" together. (Take the stone out of your shoe)

Paper- Have a concise one-page business plan and post it on the kitchen fridge.

Scissors- Identify your weaknesses and continue to improve your processes, your attitudes, and your communication until you've achieved your goals.

"Farming With Family Ain't Always Easy!"

Next Steps on Our Farm

After everyone on your farm has read this book, have a 15 minute family discussion over a coffee. Collectively identify a simple action plan for how your family can improve how you make and execute decisions together.

1/

2/

3/

4/

5/

"Farming With Family Ain't Always Easy!"

About the Author

Mark Andrew Junkin is a seventh-generation farmer, a mediator, an executive coach, a public speaker, and an author who now lives in Iowa.

Junkin grew up on his parent's farm in Bobcaygeon, Ontario, Canada and took Agriculture Business at the University of Guelph. When he went home to farm, his parents divorced after farm succession didn't go successfully. Over the last decade, Junkin has dedicated his life to developing a simple, yet radical new approach to dealing with change as it pertains to farm succession/farm management.

Junkin has been brought in by countless farm families and concerned professionals (i.e., agriculture accounting firms) to mediate the most dire farm succession crises. He has a high mediation success rate because of both his knowledge and his ability to personally relate to the farmers' situations.

In addition to mediation, Junkin offers a custom program whereby he facilitates family business meetings and provides supportive executive coach services and a team of succession experts. The "Power Hour" helps families proactively deal with change, solve problems together and focus on what matters. He started this niche practice by sitting down with local farm families throughout Ontario.

Recently, he moved just north of Iowa City, Iowa to be in the heart of the heartland. Over the past five years he has offered cost-effective services to farmers around the world via SKYPE He has clients in 14 American states, 4 Canadian provinces and a few Australians.

Junkin is also the author of a syndicated monthly column, "The Culture of Agriculture," for a growing number of farm papers

"Farming With Family Ain't Always Easy!"

across North America, Australia and Europe and has taken this theme to Live Stream where he hosts a weekly TV show on YouTube called the "Business Culture of Agriculture."

Junkin happily resides in Iowa with his wife and rapidly growing family. His wife Bernadette was a midwestern farm girl and is a major driver behind the scenes. Together they live to save family farms and have fun!

Learn more at: farmsuccession.com or call: 800 474 2057

www.ingramcontent.com/pod-product-compliance
Lightning Source LLC
Chambersburg PA
CBHW071630170526
45166CB00003B/1273